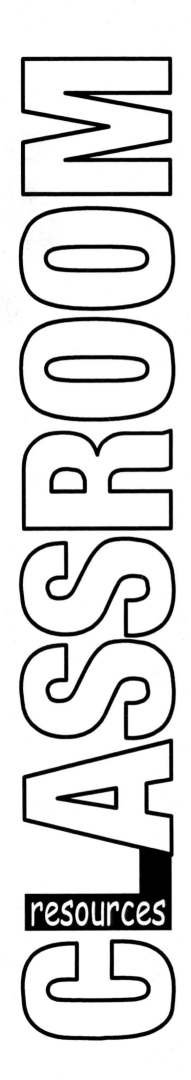

The Music Portfolio

Classical String Quartet Exercises for A-level

Published in England by

classroom resources ltd

P.O. Box 1489
Bristol
BS99 3QJ

ISBN 1 84106 108 5

This resource was written by a practising teacher

Classroom Resources Limited know that teachers work hard producing high quality resources for their own pupils. We can market those resources, ideas and innovations to other schools, colleges and academic institutions worldwide. They can benefit. You can profit.

Selling with Classroom Resources Limited costs you nothing. Simply submit your teaching ideas, photocopiable notes or software to us for review, and if we think the resource meets a need in schools then we will take care of all the production and marketing through our carefully targeted promotional literature. You will be paid royalties for every single copy we sell, we will give you higher royalties than any other publisher and you will earn an additional income for work you have already done!

For further information please contact us at:

Classroom Resources Limited
P O Box 1489
Bristol
BS99 3QJ
Tel: 0117 9406409 or Fax: 0117 9406408
Or visit our web site at:
www.classroom-resources.co.uk

Completing the Lower Parts
of a
String Quartet in the
Classical Style

A Guide for A Level Students

$*$ $*$ $*$

by

Robert Fitzgerald

COMPLETING THE LOWER THREE PARTS OF A STRING QUARTET IN THE CLASSICAL STYLE

Guidelines

It is impossible when examining the style of a composer to give a precise list of 'dos' and 'don'ts' to those who wish to imitate his or her style. The following are only guidelines which will assist in the process at this level and which will help in the avoidance of the most obvious pitfalls.

It is accepted that the late eighteenth-century string quartet reached its highest level of musical development in the hands of Haydn and Mozart. Although there are some distinctive stylistic differences between the two composers, a study of their works reveals some common traits with regard to matters of form, structure and the treatment of instruments. In order to make it easier to consult the original texts all references and exercises in this study are taken from one collection of quartets by Haydn, which should provide a sufficient introduction at this level. The source text is <u>Joseph Haydn String Quartets opp.42,50 & 54,</u> Ed. Altmann (Dover Publications).

Instrument Ranges

Violins always read from the treble clef. The viola reads from the alto C clef (occasionally the treble clef in high solo roles) with the violoncello (or 'cello) reading from the bass clef. In passages where the tessitura is constantly high it may have passages in the tenor C clef or, more rarely, the treble clef (the latter is usually reserved for prominent solo work).

The notes of the alto C clef

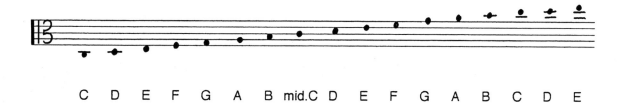

C D E F G A B mid.C D E F G A B C D E

A brief analysis of the Haydn collection shows the **working** range of the instruments to be as follows :

There are, of course, exceptions to this (see the high Violin 1 and Cello parts in Examples 1 & 2),but unless the exercises you are completing begin with an unusually high tessitura, avoid these extremes.

Example 1 : Op. 54, No. 2, 1st Movt., bars 75-77, (page 181)

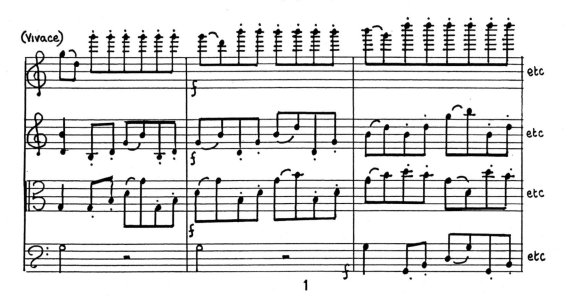

CLASSROOM resources

Example 2 : Op. 50, No. 2, 2nd Movt., bar 43-45, (page 46)

Articulation, Pizzicato and Double Stopping

Most examination boards require students to include marks of articulation etc. in their scores. Although this is not unduly complicated (a slur over a group of notes indicates that all these should be played in one bow) consider, for a moment, the difference between the following and how they might sound.

Example 3 : Different types of articulation

When including marks of articulation look carefully at the opening material to see if an obvious pattern is being established.   In the example below the first violin is required to slur across the bar line.   If this were the opening material of an examination extract, consideration would have to be given to the continuation of this method of articulation at the return or development of this (or similar) material later on.

Example 4 : Op.42, 4th Movt., bars 36-40, Violin 1 (page 11)

In general, do not introduce the instruction to pluck (*pizz.*) unless it is the opening material.   (The term *arco* informs string players to return to using the bow.)

Double and triple stopping is a special characteristic of bowed string instruments, and Haydn uses it with reasonable frequency in his quartets.   It is not always easy to execute, however, and unless you are sure that what you are writing is physically possible to play, avoid writing it altogether in examination tests. Remember that a single string can only be made to sound one note.   With the violin, viola and violoncello each having strings tuned a fifth apart thus:

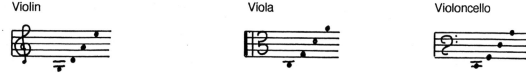

one can generally say that notes an octave or a sixth apart are reasonably safe to combine.   Some others may cause problems, however, and you are advised to keep a record of possible stoppings as you come across them.

Haydn uses double (or triple) stopping for specific reasons.   They are :
  a) to provide a fuller sound at final cadences (Example 5a & 5b),
  b) to thicken the texture in the middle parts (especially in slow movements) beneath a more
      elaborate upper part (Example 6)
  c) to add additional notes to clarify the harmony (Example 7).

Example 5a : Op.50, No.1, 1st Movt., bars 59-60 (page 15)

Example 5b : Op. 50, No.1, 4th Movt.,bars 243-245 (page 34)

Example 6 : Op. 50, No.1, 2nd Movt., bars 1 - 4 (page 21)

Example 7 : Op. 50, No.1, 3rd Movt., bars 32-36 (page 25)
(NB the double stop in the viola to introduce the Eb (i.e. the dominant 7th) at the beginning of the penultimate bar.)

Beware, however, of using double stopping in an indiscriminate fashion, especially in the form of Example 7. You should certainly be able to write good harmony using only 4 notes !

Harmonic Resource and Texture

To complete string quartets in the Classical style candidates should have a good grasp of tonal harmony, be equipped to use the dominant seventh and diminished seventh and be able to deal with prepared dissonances and elementary chromaticism, both harmonic and melodic. In most examination-type questions at least one modulation to a nearly related key will be expected.

On the whole the texture of the examination-type quartet will be predominantly homophonic, with clearly defined phrases and cadence points. Candidates should be aware, however, of the importance of writing individual lines which may include moments of rest and short imitative figures. An ability to take a given motive and apply it consistently throughout a subsequent chord progression is essential as is the ability to recognise harmony notes and non-harmonic tones in a given melody.

Look at the following extract from the opening movement of Op.42 in D minor.

Example 8 : Op.42, 1st Movt., bars 1-8 (page 1)

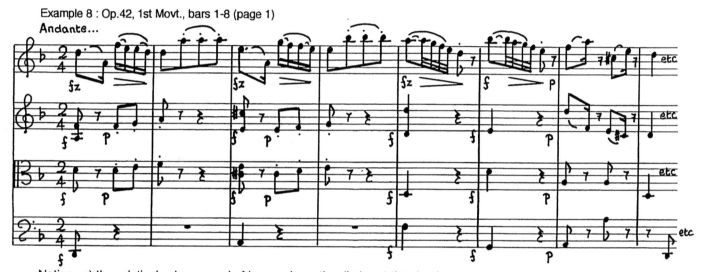

Notice a) the relatively slow speed of harmonic motion (in bar 4 the dominant seventh sounded in bar 3 receives further dissonance with the addition of the ninth in Violin 1.)
b) the clarity of the harmony
c) the clear cadential progression Ic - V - I
d) the decoration of the melodic line with anticipations and passing notes
e) the variety of texture ranging from 6 notes (bar 3, beat 1) to a single note (bar 4, beat 2)
f) the density and spacing of the instruments (spanning a full three octaves at its widest).

Look at the extract below which is from the last movement of the same quartet.

Example 9 : Op.42, 4th Movt., bars 41 - 47(page 11)

Notice a) the slow speed of harmonic motion (a D major triad with the addition of the seventh from bar 43)

b) the movement of the 'cello under the chords in the upper three instruments

c) the movement of the instruments in thirds or sixths apart using a consistent motive with the rhythm :

d) textural variety through antiphony between pairs of instruments.

Melodic Dissonance

The characteristic features of melodic composition in the Classical period can be summarised as :

a)   clear periodicity (i.e. phrases clearly marked with cadences and a 'feel' of rest)

b)   a preference for the antecedent/consequent phrase pattern (i.e. a phrase which ends on the dominant chord is 'answered' by a phrase of the same or roughly equal length ending on the tonic.)

c)   a preference for phrases or motives of two or four bars in length

d)   a controlled, but frequent use, of non-harmonic tones to elaborate what are otherwise 'harmonically-charged' melodic ideas (i.e. those which clearly outline or suggest a harmonic progression).

In harmonising with lower strings a melody from this period the candidate must be aware of the above and be able to identify the cadences and the implied harmony.   Whereas the first can be straightforward the second sometimes causes problems.   Here is a summary of the most commonly used non-harmonic tones.

Example 10 : The Passing Note (unaccented)

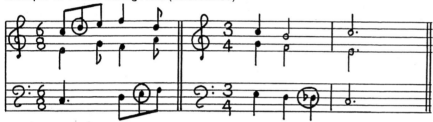

Example 11 : The Passing Note (accented)

Example 12 : The Upper and Lower Auxiliary (NB Haydn's fondness for the Chromatic version in Example 12)

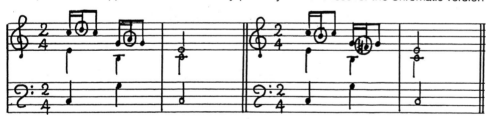

Example 13 : Op.54, No.1, 1st Movt., bar 118 (page 162)

5

The appoggiatura is frequently used and is one of the chief causes of the misunderstanding by pupils of the implied harmony. The appoggiatura should, by definition, be approached by step and move to the nearest harmony note, thus :

Example 14 : The Appoggiatura

Example 15a and 15b offer two further examples. Note that in 15a the dissonance is compounded further with the cello remaining on C natural as a pedal under the chromatic appoggiatura rather than moving to B natural thereby creating Chord V7b.

Example 15a : Chromatic appoggiatura in violin I Op 54, No.1, 2nd Movt., bars 71 -72 (page 166)

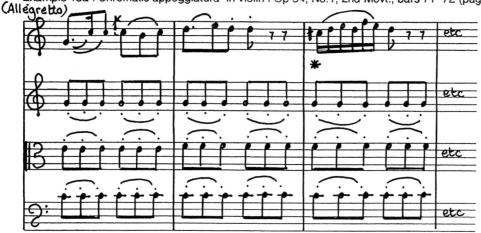

Example 15b : Chromatic turns in violin I and cello : Op.50, No.4, 3rd Movt., bars 8 - 11 (page 97)

Sometimes 2 or more appoggiaturas may be combined, especially at a cadence, as in Example 16. (Strictly speaking the A in violin II is a suspension, not an appoggiatura, because of its preparation.) The effect is to produce a Ic - V chord progression known as a **feminine cadence**.

Example 16 : Op.50, No.4, 2nd Movt., bars 3-4 (page 92)

6

This cadential decoration was frequently used during the Pre-Classical, Classical and Romantic Periods. It can also be introduced onto the final chord of a perfect cadence as in Example 17. In this case the 2 'appoggiaturas' are combined with a **retardation of the leading note**, all of which is dissonant to the cello on the first beat of the bar.

Example 17 : Op.50, No.4, 2nd Movt., bars 7-8 (page 92)

Other common non-harmonic tones are :

a) the Échappée b) Changing notes and c) the Anticipation.

Example 18 :

The Échappée   Changing Notes   The Anticipation.

EXERCISE 1

Give an harmonic analysis of the following extract from Op.50, No.1, 4th Movt. bars 1 - 8 (page 27). Write the chords/figures underneath. Circle all non-harmonic tones in violin I and identify them.

1.   Op.50, No.1, 4th Movt. bars 1 - 8 (page 27)

CLASSROOM

EXERCISE 2

Map out with a single bass note and numbers/figures a likely harmonisation for these violin I melodies. Circle the non-harmonic tones and identify them.

1.   Op.50, No.3, 4th Movt., bars 1 - 12 (page 77)

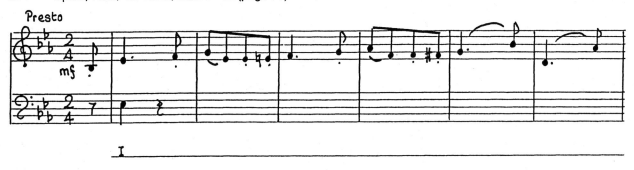

2.   Op.50, No.6, 3rd Movt., bars 32-44 (Trio) (page 143)

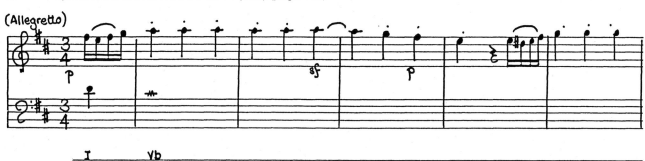

EXERCISE 3

.1.   Complete in 4-part harmony these cadential progressions.   Include in each a feminine ending.

CLASSROOM

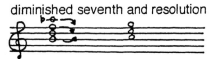

The Diminished Seventh and II7b 'chromatic'

The general 'rule' for the use of the diminished triads formed on the 7th degree of the scale in major keys and on the 7th (if sharpened) and 2nd degrees of the scale in minor keys holds good for all pre-classical and classical quartets, i.e. **use them only in the first inversion**. There are, of course, numerous exceptions, but to avoid learning some additional rules for preparation and resolution it is better simply to find another chord.

The diminished *seventh* chord can be imagined as being a *dominant* minor ninth, but without a root thus :

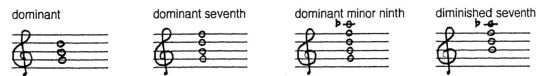

As such, its natural resolution should be onto **chord I.** Although other resolutions are possible, it is unlikely that they will be required in the examination.

diminished seventh and resolution

Look at the diminished sevenths in Examples 19a and 19b below. Although in both cases the chord I is not the tonic of the movement, the diminished seventh will be used correctly if you treat it as such, allowing the interval of the diminished seventh (or augmented second when inverted) to resolve correctly :

Ex. 19a: Op.54, No.2, 3rd Movt., bars 54 - 56 (page 192)

Ex. 19b : Op.50, No.1, 3rd Movt., bars 18 - 20 (page 25)

Candidates should acquaint themselves with the Neapolitan Sixth and German Sixth (See **A Level Harmony** by the same author) as chords occasionally found in Haydn's work, as well as the more common sharpening of the third in chord II (the Chromatic Supertonic) in the first inversion just before chord V7 of a perfect cadence (NB. not to use the 7th in chord V would imply modulation, so be careful!) e.g.

Example 20 : Op.50, No.3, 1st Movt., bars 26-29 (page 62)

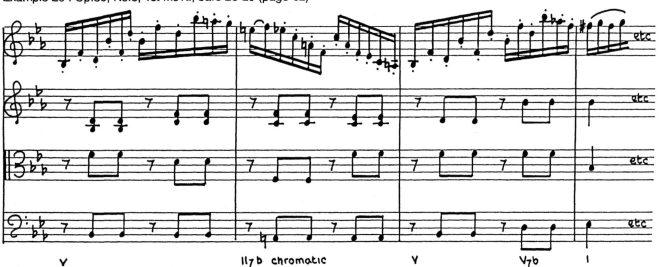

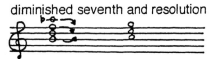

9

Speed of Harmonic Motion

In general Haydn attempts to harmonise every beat of a bar only when creating a serious and majestic mood. At other times the rate of harmonic change can be relatively slow (i.e. one or two chords per bar in triple-time movements, one or two chords per bar in quadruple-time movements), though in articulating cadence points there is often a noticeable increase. Candidates should strive in their answers to maintain a slow rate of chord change especially when the underlying parts are accompanying a lyrical upper part.

The Pedal

Pedals play an important role in increasing tension and occur frequently both in the bass and in the upper parts as in examples 13 and 15a above. They may also occur in violin II or the viola as in example 6. It is difficult to give guidelines about when to use them, since with the violin I line as the 'given' line much will depend upon its direction.

Pedals, whether sustained or reiterated, are generally employed on the tonic or dominant notes in anticipation of a cadence (it is often good to think of dominant pedals as an extension of the Ic chord before the perfect cadence and tonic pedals as codas following a perfect or interrupted cadence. An important rule, however, is that pedals should always begin as a harmony note and generally end as such. One possibility for incorporating a pedal in your exercises is to have simultaneous pedals in violin I and cello (as long as there is sufficient movement elsewhere), e.g.

Example 21: A pedal in violin I and cello : Op.50, No.1, 1st Movt., bars 55 - 58 (page 15)

String Figurations

It is impossible in his short analysis paper to investigate the enormous variety of accompanimental figurations which Haydn uses. From the examples given so far the candidate should begin to appreciate how Haydn 'cultivates' the two elements of clarity and simplicity. The candidate is strongly advised to consult as many original texts as possible to assimilate the style and to make a 'vocabulary' list of the types of figurations which occur most frequently.

* * * * *

Hints for working examination-style exercises.

1. Remember the golden rule that a simple harmonisation is best. Use chords I, IV and V whenever possible to give good clear harmonic direction.
2. Remember. Chord V should be followed by I (or VI)
3. Use a slow rate of harmonic change unless the opening suggests otherwise.
4. Be prepared for some chromatic movement. Know how to use the chromatic chords mentioned above. (See **A Level Harmony** by the same author.)

5. Identify the cadence points and use the standard progressions, e.g. Ic - V - I or IIb - V7 - I. Be prepared to use feminine endings if the melody suggests them.
6. Examine the given melody and identify the non-harmonic tones. Sketch out the harmonic framework and add the bass before filling in the inner parts. Look at the possibility of a pedal.
7. Remember to write for STRINGS, not a piano on 4 staves. (A well-spaced string quartet rarely lies comfortably for two hands at the keyboard.) Look at the opening material for clues about the figurations and be consistent in their employment. Examine the motive on which a particular figuration is based and be prepared to adapt it as necessary. (Some pieces might well require more than one type of figuration or even passages in octaves, so be careful!)
8. The anacrusis in the Classical period is frequently left unharmonised. Check with the opening material for guidance.
9. Add marks of articulation and expression to all parts **under** the relevant stave.
10. If not a first study viola player check your viola part very carefully.

EXERCISES

Complete the exercises below adding the second violin, viola and cello parts. The first violin is given in full. Add marks of articulation and expression to your work.

Ex.1 *Op.50, No.3, 4th Movt., bars 1 - 12 (page 77)*
This completes the inner parts of Exercise 2 (1) (page 8) in which the cello only was sketched out. Maintain the opening rhythm in violin II and viola until bar 8. End with an imperfect cadence.

Ex.2 *Op.54, No.1, 4th Movt., bars 18 - 26 (page 172) &*
Op.54, No.1, 4th Movt., bars 1 - 8 (page 171)
Treat as two exercises. Complete using, first, violin melody a) ending in the tonic and, second, violin melody b) modulating to the dominant.

Ex.3 *Op.50, No.5, 4th Movt., bars 1 - 12 (page 119)*
Keep violin II above violin I for one more bar.

Ex.4 *Op.54, No.1, 3rd Movt., bars 1 - 10 (page 169)*
Watch out! 5-bar phrases.

Ex.5 *Op.50, No.2, 3rd Movt., (Trio) bars 51 - 66 (page 49)*
End first half and final cadence in the dominant. Put arpeggio material in the cello immediately after the half bar and let violins move in thirds.

Ex.6 *Op.50, No.2, 2nd Movt., bars 1 - 8 (page 44)*
The b natural in bar 6 is a chromatic appoggiatura. Violin I stays below violin II throughout.

Ex.7 *Op.54, No.2, 2nd Movt., bars 1 - 8 (page 188)*
Adopt a chordal style (harmonic rate of change at the crotchet) ending in dominant.

Ex.8 *Op.42, 3rd Movt., bars 1 - 12 (page 8)*
Maintain the opening style and conclude with a feminine ending.

Ex.9 *Op.42, 2nd Movt., (Trio) (page 7)*
Modulate to the relative major at the end of the first half.

Ex.10 *Op.54, No.1, 4th Movt., bars 26 - 40 (page 172)*
Lighten the texture of the lower parts once the violin begins to move in semiquavers. End in the relative major.

Ex.11 *Op.54, No.2, 3rd Movt., bars 1 - 8 (page 191)*

Ex.12 *Op.54, No.2, 4th Movt., Bras 8 - 16 (page 193)*
Very slow quaver pulse. Maintain arched quaver movement in the cello with semiquavers in the other parts. The bracket and the figure 2 at the beginning allude to the fact that this extract begins in a second-time bar. The time signature is 2/4.

Ex.13 *Op.54, No.3, 3rd Movt., (Trio) (page 216)*
End with an imperfect cadence.

EXERCISE 1

EXERCISE 2

EXERCISE 3

EXERCISE 4

EXERCISE 5

EXERCISE 6

EXERCISE 7

EXERCISE 8

EXERCISE 9

EXERCISE 10

EXERCISE 11

Allegretto

EXERCISE 12

EXERCISE 13

18

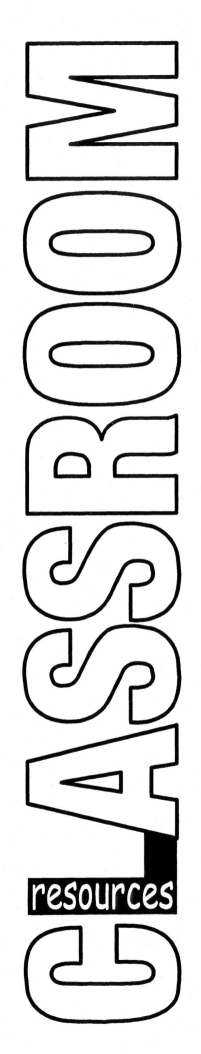

The Music Portfolio

Classical String Quartet Exercises for A-level

CLASSROOM resources

operates a programme of constant improvement and updating of its resources.

If you have any comments to make on this resource, please complete this page and return it to us at

POB 1489, Bristol BS99 3JQ

Please place a cross on each line at a point which best indicates your response to the question above it.

How pleased are you with this resource?

not at all   very

Does this resource represent good value for money?

not at all   very

Would you buy more material from classroom resources?

definitely not   definitely

Please make any specific comments you have in the space provided below (continue overleaf if necessary):

<u>About you (optional)</u>

Tick this box if you require further information about Classroom Resources ☐

School name:

Address:

Your name:

Position in School:

Thank you